Machine Dreams, Macabre Awakenings®

Choice Poetry, Spring 2015

Penned By: JRF Bacon III

Machine Dreams, Macabre Awakenings

Type:
Copyright
Registration Number:
1124132
Status:
Registered
Registered:
2015-09-02
ISBN:
978-0-9949006-0-9

Cover photo by A Fine Line Designs & Photography
Makeup by Jessi Lee Smith
Arranged by M. Swift Stephen

Table of Contents

23. Fireflies on Wings of Night (12 May 2015)
24. Severed Ties (7 May 2015)
25. Death Alight (17 Jun 2015)
26. Fettered Soul (8 May 2015)
27. Spring (12 May 2015)
28. Spring cont. (12 May 2015)
29. Spring cont. (12 May 2015)
30. Sunsnuffer (6 May 2015)
31. Slumberdust (24 May 2015)
32. Mold (10 Jun 2015)
33. Chasing Night (9 Jun 2015)
34. Cat Corral (5 Jun 2015)
35. Buried (25 May 2015)
36. Jailed (27 May 2015)
37. Selfish Breath (29 May 2015)
38. Cheshire's Mist (28 Jun 2015)
39. Forsake (26 May 2015)
40. Rushing Fear (28 May 2015)
41. Crush (25 May 2015)
42. Luxe (2 Jul 2015)
43. Tall Tales (4 Jun 2015)
44. Fogs of Dream (2 Jul 2015)
45. Madness Blind (2 Jul 2015)
46. Promethean Fire (7 Jul 2015)
47. All That You Revere (3 Jul 2015)
48. Victorious (8 Jul 2015)
49. Malaria & Love (5 Jul 2015)
50. Bourgeois & Lioness (9 Jul 2015)
51. Soils of Despair (7 Jul 2015)
52. Genius-Wings (30 Jun 2015)
53. Velvet Breeze (7 Jul 2015)

JRF Bacon III

For you.

Judge

So very brave
an open heart
this naked ink
this burning star
it gives no fucks
it turns to stone
it levels blood and dust
and bone
I see your eyes
pour o'er my soul
you judge with hammer
gavel's toll
I turn my flesh
to death, to ice
I listen never
once, twice, thrice

Apex

I buy whiskey
and breathe fire
I melt the change
and forge spades
I dig these stones
it rains diamonds
I loot the skies
I dodge demise
I realize where nihilism lies

Dread & Pigs

The sun is sinking low and orange
when this light slips away
my brain will scatter
like cockroaches in incandescence
we dread the mornings
we dread these police
blind guard-dogs of slavery
wagging for bones on these city streets

Unholy

And fail you may
and die you might
and living through
unholy light
and marching down
and leading on
and drumming loud
unholy song
and lightning strikes
and lightning twice
and fires burn bright
unholy night
and sitting cold
and gloaming still
and thriving in
unholy will

Through Blood

These flags fly high
these drums dig deep
through fogs of war that ne'er do sleep

they rumble low
they tremor still
through generations of conflicting will

this sky is mine
this holy land
through salvation he will force my hand

to ending reigns
to slaughtered foes
through the night we'd drink our battle-woes

and living still
and thriving not
through our sons' blood 'tis not forgot

so onwards now
so onwards then
through sacrifice we'll bring an end

to bleeding out
to bleeding dry
through blood we'll claim this holy sky

Machine Dreams, Macabre Awakenings

I turn my cheek from this mothering of greed
in the cradle of alchemy
this darkness will usurp the throne
of these steel-woven dreams
I will walk on these machines
these machines in the sky
the cloud-builders
the sun-chariots
I will walk into their dreams
and bleed the rivets from their seams
they will talk to me like kings
and they will fall for me like queens
with a kiss upon the cheek, be turned
and lessons never – books be burned
this ashen knowledge ne'er to glow
this river's darkened everflow

Poison Dart

"With this ring, I thee wed"
the flowers on your final bed
"Both in sickness, and in health"
I lift the veil from your cold mouth
"Until death do us part"
a six-foot pit, a poison dart
"I now pronounce you man and wife"
this promise of eternal life
"You may now kiss the bride"
I raise the blade and climb inside

New World

Oblivious in this new world
where wonder overtakes us
and the crypt smiles in wait
with its stone jaws
jagged in the sky
reaching its dead to the stars

Trampled Flowers

Watering this soul
praying for these trampled flowers
I died last night
and poisoned these gardens
I'm through with this light
I hold its head beneath oceans of wine
and I watch these flowers die

Sinking Deep in Darkness Made

These fairy-tales in moonlight, brooding
fanged devils dance in circles, looming
round fires of midnight's silence, blooming
the flowers of sacrifice bladed, pruning

and here amidst its thinning airs
where sights grow dim, where eyes despair
this void of light does softly lurk
both in the tomb and on the hearth

it plucks the stars from black-ink skies
it pulls the moon with magnet eyes
this silver scythe, the crescent blade
sinking deep in darkness made

Rosy

Sometimes I wish I was insane
and everything was rosy
a pocket full of posies
and smiling down the lane

I Will Never Come Back Home

We stripped her bones
next to the thundering spring torrent
she shot orange suns into the night
she shot wonder burning bright
the white foam frothing on moonlight
where the forest's silhouette breaks the sky
I extend my hand and ask why
I shield my face I pretend to die
this means nothing to me
and I will never come back home
I will fuck your daughters
and all of Rome

Vengeance

I still draw breath
I hold your demons close
I dig graves for the choicest angels
I sing a song of death; morose
I walk the edge of the sky
I remember your smile
I set these clouds on fire with haunting desire
I watch scorched feathers rain for miles

Forever's Wall

The day is near
when waking ends
the final sun sets
clouds un-mend
mirrors glazed
within the skull
escaping now
in twilight's lull
this path is walked
is walked alone
footfalls o'er
a heaven's roam
all for naught
and naught for all
no trace cut
on Forever's wall

Siren's Rim

Parasitic spirit-feed
hosted sucker evil-breed
she smiles in dance
a trance with look
she sinks her unrelenting hooks
she'll push you out
she'll draw you in
she ebbs and flows
the tides of sin
enclosing sails
in luring winds
she drags you near
the Siren's rim
and crashing hard
upon the shores
and bleeding dry
a love abhorred

Wolf & Crow

The lone wolf rumbles
black and green
on forest floors
the hunter's dream
fangs are rearing
blades of fright
blood of prey
in pale moonlight
flashing sinking
low in flesh
and spraying life
malevolent
steaming frothing
on the snow
letting howls
betwixt the crows
flying high
round carcass still
diving into
brother's kill
a darkened kin
a secret bond
of wing and paw
on frost and pond
on shoulders wide
and perched thereon
ever-feeding
carrion

Disciples Nine

There is no light
these tunnels we search
blind beneath daylight
fed darkness in church
and we eat from the hand
of this old feeble man
he feigns certainty
this divinity spell
pushing draughts from its well
he poisons children
he keeps old junkies
the spirit-pusher
the decrepit tool
carving breads and spilling wine
between the lips, disciples nine
minus three, the trinity
we bleed the holy corps d'esprit

False-Borne Skies

Yes this heart is bleeding still
from chasms of a death-blown quill
the ink that seeps into the soul
and poisons minds beyond control
it makes them quake and gnash and kill
it makes them fight against their will
propaganda gears be greased
the devil's false-borne skies unleashed

Down

Cursed
daily by this open firmament
this gravity keeps me still
infinity taunts
my wings do nothing
my feet are sucked down
I've never felt so heavy
I gaze long into this abyss
and I am emptied
this eternity
is pulling me
down

Where the Wicked Soul Sleeps

When born again
outlawed
and freedom is king
no desire for the future
this moment
fuel of instinct
one ignites
naked
unashamed
already caged
already maimed
already dead
now you taste life
now you breathe deep
there is no rest
where the wicked soul sleeps

Caged Snakes

These mighty caged snakes
their silent breath through steel bars
slithering their release
the day dies in fires of industry
through fixed locks and barbed wire
vagabond wolves, dire
freedom dries dank
on the lines in the midnight sun
it cradles death in everyone
spears soaked in night's cloak
striking true
down forgotten avenues - ghost town blues
at the crossroads paying devil's dues

Flittermice & Sheep

Silence creeping
lost in dream
echoed death
of Nazarene
blinded blood-fold
crimson crown
they follow fools
throughout the town
the flittermice
lead droves of sheep
the blind lead dumb
from cliffs of sleep
and towing ropes
round limp-flung throats
the snake constricts
the demon bloats

Fireflies on Wings of Night

Fireflies on wings of night
flashing hopeless sparks of sight
candles in abysmal dark
throw no light on wonder's art
forever now this blackness grows
and reaches out where no light throws
tapers dwindle downwards shine
pulling heaven's flame divine
into pits where silence weaves
the footfalls of disease it breathes
flashing hopeless sparks of sight
fireflies on wings of night

Severed Ties

Severed ties
the trumpets blow
enemies gather
'neath walls below
hatred waxes
love, it wanes
in bleeding hearts
this vengeance reigns
a beast of steel
in hands I'd loved
now sinks its fangs
into my glove
this hollow horror
drains my soul
these eyes I'd loved
without control
now slings a fletch
with razor grief
to sever hearts
in disbelief

Death Alight

Fuck the sun
give me night
give me wonder
death alight
drop the pill
raven's quill
black ink pools
in eyes unstill
sucking light
from mother sun
dripping fire
on devil's drum
rumble low
on dead man's row
skeleton feet
in rattled-toe
on death-march bleak
on raven's beak
on silvered blades
in backs of sleep
sink now slow
hot blood on snow
crimson streams
bring death in throes
and lie now still
on raven's quill
and dire breath
breathes pyre's will

Fettered Soul

I drink to death
with lips of bone
I drink the sun of twilight's drone
I sip the fire
I brandish woe
I sleep beneath the devil's row
with cloven hooves
a thunder laid
debts of dead-eyed coins been paid
to ferry me
between these worlds
released
my fettered soul unfurls

Spring

Spring is here
and I crawl from my cave
counting all the coins I've saved
onto the peaks of mountains to take in the sun
and the blue skies pain my eyes
I yearn for the return of winter
I wish you would all crawl back in your holes
un-sunlit and battered; shattered
unclean and unwavering
cabin-fevered death defiers
town criers
liars
slaves and pyres
weakening the asphalt still
mining trucks destroying tax bucks
it's always past my bedtime
I always crave red wine
I will leave you all aghast
jaws agape in wait
the next trip of fate
your sullied slate
you kill everything
the loose joint
the weak link
floorboards groaning underfoot
and fireplace awash with soot
I paint my face and rob your banks
I steal your wives and spank, spank, spank
and whistling a graveyard tune

I watch you die beneath the moon
this shovel strikes the earth again
my body aches
I want this end
I should have faked my death
joined the priesthood
pretended to be good
but drink the wine and eat the wafers
never sell an ounce to beggars
when I look up at these stars
they shine
nothing beats this
and I could die
we blink at each other
they are my brothers
and I know I will never die alone when it's night
in this devil's maze, the stargaze
this body will crumble
your walls will tumble
these flags will burn
they mean nothing
invisible borders
and you gather at rallies
in back alleys
you spread fear and kill cheer
you are the merchants of doom
you open tombs
you walk the earth
in never-ending search
of gold
you'd steal it from a baby's hold
there is a sickness in your halls
armoured in red tape
watch the birdie

don't look at me
we've set you free
pay me
I'll keep you blind in your seat
defeat
I don't care about your ways
this haze
nothing matters
these castles will crumble
the earth will flame
unashamed
and nothing is forever
even diamonds wait to die
your never-ending vows are drunk
by black holes in the sky

Sunsnuffer

These scars in twilight
milestone strife
where darkness licked my heels with knives
and narrowly escaping doors
snuffing suns forevermore
I steal light through faults of hope
I grip my last fistful of rope
it sees me through another day
these shafts of light, the sombre-slay
while round and round these birds of prey
circle winds of darkest grey
pressing weaker spirits still
sucking life and love and will
and pulled into the cyclone's eye
this calm that lulls the need to die
while birds of prey go sailing o'er
snuffing suns forevermore

Slumberdust

Soaring on polluted night
wisdom's ghost
in treetop flight
spanning aeons – slumberdust
waking mountains – Saturnlust
winged lions of the sky
kings of jungled starlight fly
reigning high above the peaks
in silence soaring ne'er to speak
the mystic secret of these groves
the pulse nocturne, in rhythmic droves
flowing through the heart of night
soaring on polluted light

Mold

The grip, the hold
this sacred mold
collective oppression
they tighten the fold
the elite discreet
between the sheets
hammering deals
for winks and treats
to sell your soul
your bell it tolls
they've pulled the rug
beneath your toes
they dribble coins
they heat your loins
you watch the bird
you come unjoined
now pry your eyes
now heads to skies
now trust you not
the treacherous lies

Chasing Night

Tailing demons
chasing night
hellbound moths
in hellfire light
followed down
to flowing springs
of poisoned wells
flap leathered wings
they lead now far
from earthen glows
far from breezes
soft and slow
far from sunrise
and sunset
far from quarrels
song and jest
and deeper still
the devil's tomb
the very slit
of Satan's womb
fly now forth
the newborn son
on winds of darkness
run now, run

Cat Corral

You draw the line
you raise the flag
you litter the land
with hired dogs
dropouts
dope-fiends
above the law
corralling cats
with blackjack bats
skewed watchmen
in the night
demand respect
in unearned vests
they stand for nothing
but their paycheck

Buried

Midnight-jeweled thrusting spades
see earth and air reversed, displaced
a crevasse dug in passion-throes
a sleepless life of nightmare's woes
this blood red shade before my eyes
has warred my soul, has sent to die
the lover's heart within this chest
the turning of my cheek for best
and entropy leaves not untouched
this love that was for so long crutched
by brighter days by joyous song
for years these shoulders brushing wrongs
and crumbled now to flattened earth
true north is spinning on the hearth
it's spitting fire it's spitting rage
it's fuelling this very spade
which thrusting deep in midnight's jewel
now burns the last days of the fool

Jailed

Jailed vermin
jailed prince
jailed water
jailed winds
jail the common passerby
jail the apple of our eye
jailed forest
jailed moor
jailed satyr
jail doors
shutting out the light of day
shutting all to our dismay
jailed jailers in the hall
jailed wardens, toppled; all
jailed judges
jailed priests
jailed lovers
jailed creeps
jail everything that moves
jail everything in you

Selfish Breath

I drift
I sway
I've sailed away
inside myself
the soldier slouched
these bullets rain
on the dirt
unspent and heavy
I fall to my knees,
I kneel for none but me
there is no weakness in this death
no single selfish breath

Cheshire's Mist

Winter forced
through frigid bone
blizzard tunneled
zombie drone
steals you from Goliath's fist
sneaks you down
on Cheshire's mist
plunging tower
deep inside
aligning cosmic silenced bride
honouring our cherished dead
dancing on eternal beds
forcing winter
forcing night
chasing suns from risen sight
closing rolling stones of doom
a fortnight working serpent's loom
fabrics from a heaven's fall
weaving cloth for reaper's pall
draped now black on final tomb
where death has died
and corpse exhumed
by puller of celestial threads
the puppeteer's unbroken bread

Forsake

These dreary oars
pull on glass
cut through mist
on the devil's pass
candle lit
on lanterned bow
watered cross
upon her brow
and teeming in
my faintest wake
the heart of all
that I forsake
the closeness of
a tender form
a warmth within
the coldest morn
I sail them down
this ancient lake
the heart of all
that I forsake

Rushing Fear

I can't surface
I am a slug
dealing death blows
with dagger eyes
I am a vacuum
empty
pulling at you all
I pull this shank
from deafness
I rush these words
into your ear:
you need fear
the end is near

Crush

I blink now once
I push the light
I blink now twice
and it is night
I close my eyes
and see it rain
these butterflies
they flutter pain
and storming seas
a world away
a single flap
a plague astray
ever seeming silent - still
ever crushing strongest will

Luxe

Surf the flux and fuck the luxe
burning all temptation's took
finest silks and platinum stores
debauchery with Jesus' whores
ride the wave into the grave
steamroll jets and break champagnes
grounding business moguls now
in the muck and milking cows
pulling steel from the sky
dagger in temptation's eye
in garden's grown and furs be worn
shame-paint and sweatshops unborn

Tall Tales

Come closer
share this sacred gift
we dive from bridges
left to right
jump from traffic
take flight
leave these machines
rusted in awakened wakes
the collective quakes
the tremors of rage
turn the page
un-inked red tape
unwound from justice' nape
these scales
balanced invisible whales
where tall tales failed the holy grail

Fogs of Dream

Treading heavy
on the meniscus of dream
thunderous pounding
souls unseamed
skeletons prying
let themselves through
on to leech and ruin you
the great eye that never sleeps
above us all
on concrete streets
watching every breath and pace
every coin that lends is traced
so pound now through the walls of dream
escape into the northern gleam
launder clean the gold you've made
blind the eye, in comfort lay
down beside the banks of blue
rushing slumber unto you
so fall now through
the fogs of dream
so fall now far
awakened be

Madness Blind

I've let them out
the eyes, the lives
I've killed them all
they've plead and died
I've shed not yet
a single tear
I've shed this flesh
six times per year
and I will never let you know
from where this darkness forth does flow
where madness hidden
madness blind
you cannot kill
what you can't find

Promethean Fire

Is the hour not now close at hand
this radar blip, this flash of pan
and derelict of forcing light
into outlooks - onward, bright
and we dig into the dust
reaping thoughts and wonderlust
of these blazing stars of ours
Promethean fire in our hearts
a thousand torches passed for naught
for all humanity's hammers wrought
this ball of dust we toil and dig
this ball of dust - the human brig
it will not stand the test of time
the pan is flashing bright, sublime

All That You Revere

I am not in here alone
in this shell of flesh and bone
it walks with me
it leads my stride
it's toed me o'er these oceans wide
it's seen me down from heavens high
it's forced a spear into my side
and down the winding stair of Hell
it's clipped my wing
and tolled my bell
it bears the light
for all mankind
this fallen angel never lies
it shows me truth
it does not fear
it questions all that you revere

Victorious

I've juiced the noonday sun
squeezing fire in my cup
I leave your czars in a swath of stars
as the pale moon goes dark
nothing grows
but winter snows
and frigid bones
Death is crowned victorious
Death who drank the sun
Death who walks the frozen plains
sipping fire - all but one

Malaria & Love

Stagnant
this blood pools
mosquitoes swarm
the deaf drone
I lie still
I let them drink
deep in thoughts of sadness - sink
unwanted and chained
drained and slain
all that is left to live for
is meaningless to me
I do love you
but I'm so jaded
and this path is deadly
monotone poisons
flow in its ditches
this thirst is unbearable
this dream ends tonight

Bourgeois & Lioness

This time things will be different
the afterglow burns low
in the fierce flow
of woman scorned
she will undo your first born
this time things will be different
this raft won't come apart
right off the start
in the undertow
of a woman scorned
in the fierce flow
of the undone, borne
in that maelstrom
of heavens, wet
fear the bourgeois, fear the lioness

Soils of Despair

Nothing lies 'tween you and me
but the lies that bore
the fruit of this tree
grown in soils of despair
we fed it riches that were not there
and felling now, limb from limb
a hollowed trunk and branches thin
an illusion of a tree that be
soaking in sunlight for we
and lying now there on the grass
this love has finally died at last
fed from lies and dark deceit
the kiss of tree bark at our feet

Genius-Wings

Careful-footed, deliberate
stranglehold on the throats of decadence
this wave heaves forth
built on the shoulders of brilliance
forebears of forgotten ways
these petty crooks
these drones
surviving under genius-wings
with their insignificant shadows
feeding the machine
this wave crashes down
abandoning righteous paths
to press their teeth in tests of gold

Velvet Breeze

The cloud thickens on this sunrise
it holds us all and rests our eyes
the bones dance on ivory keys
the fleshless touch of velvet breeze
she plays to us, she lulls from sleep
the footfalls of uncounted sheep
and there inside her black-hole pits
the sockets where her sight would sit
were slowly whirling pools of wind
hypnotic, mesmerizing, grim
swirling with the haunting tones
pressed from under ivory, bone
pulls each one of us inside
alive, against our will, we fly
down into those tunneled winds
forever reaching deep within
and on into the storm's black eye
where letting go and down we lie
before the row of ivory keys
play haunting tones of velvet breeze

About the Author

Joe Bacon III is a musician, songwriter,
artist and poet. A member of the Canadian Forces
from 2002-2006 Joe has been writing poetry since
1990 and has developed an extensive and diverse
collection of work. Born and raised in Sudbury he
has lived in Calgary, Halifax and Toronto and
currently divides his time between Sudbury and
his camp in the Muskoka region of Ontario.

www.ingramcontent.com/pod-product-compliance
Lightning Source LLC
Chambersburg PA
CBHW060538030426

42337CB00021B/4329